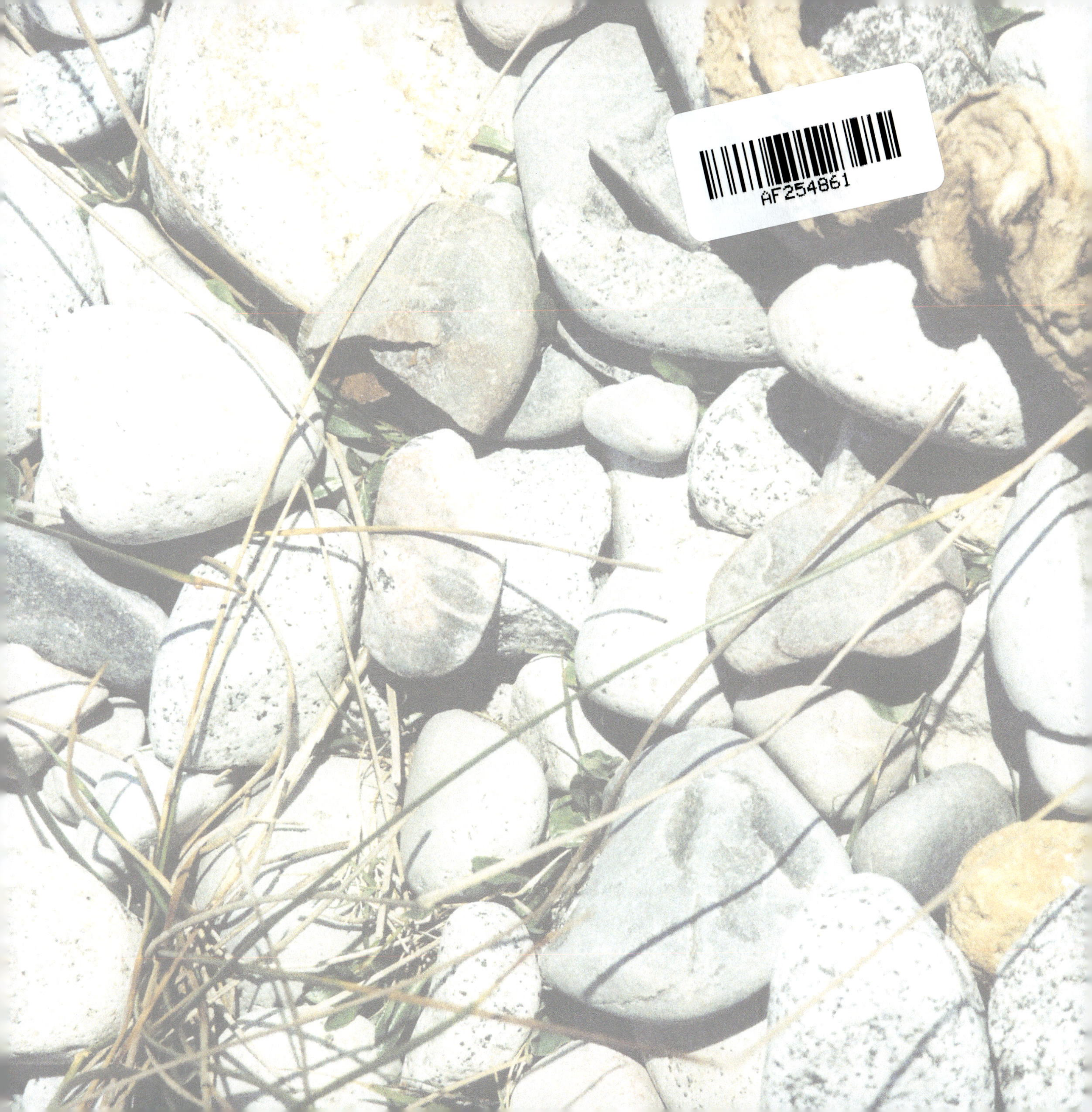

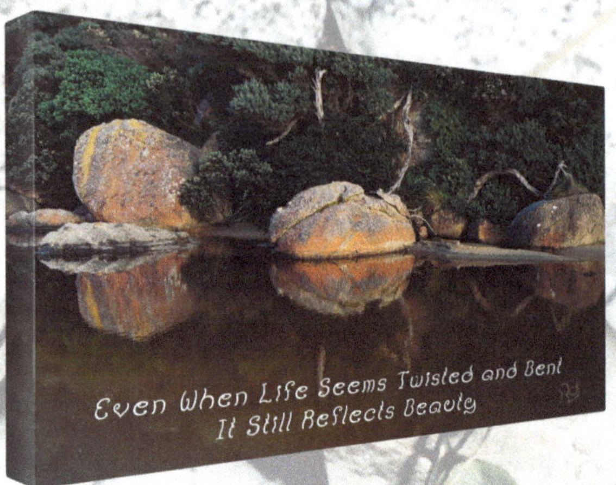

Matching Canvas Wall Print

This professionally printed and finished fine art canvas, will create a feeling of tranquillity and inspire hope.

Available for purchase with or without the inspirational quote, completing a book and print set.

Each high quality and unique print, features the artists own photography, quote and signature.

To purchase this matching canvas wall print or view other signed artwork, visit www.pebblecollections.com for details.

Pebble Poetry Series thus far

...

Pebble or Pearl

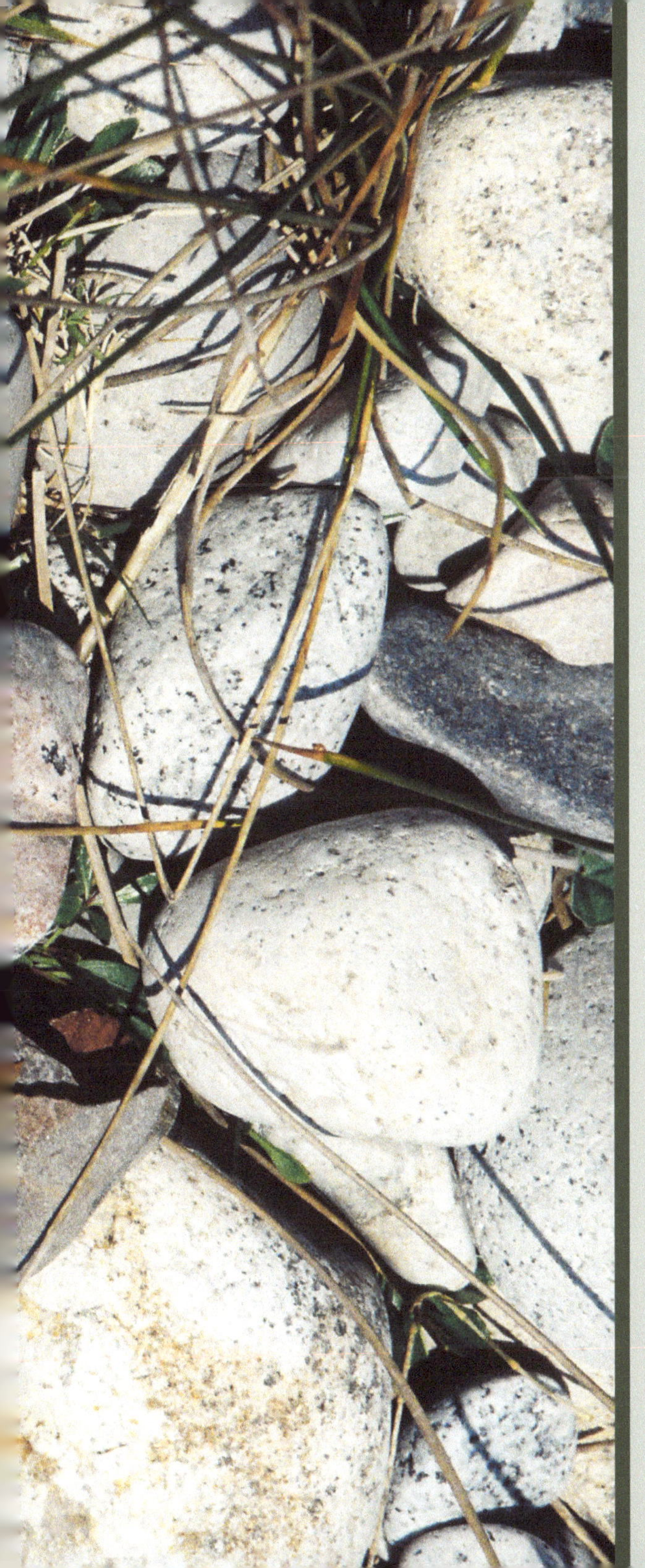

PEBBLE POETRY

Pebble or Pearl

POEMS & ILLUSTRATIONS BY

Ruth Parfett

POET, ARTIST & PHOTOGRAPHER

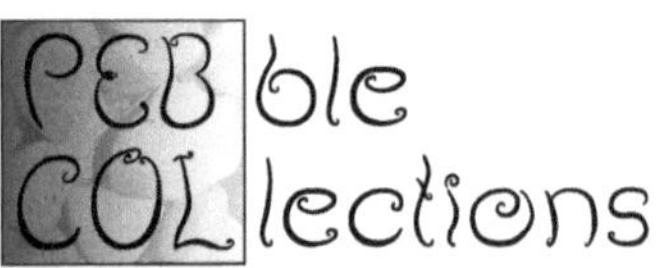

www.pebblecollections.com

Fore*poem*

Penned during life, for life
Each pebble inspired by those I care
Founded from experiences I have had
Bound for you to share

Times of trial and stress
Are like broken pebbles in your shoe
Sharp, rough and aggravating
Making it hard to see things through

It's easy to ignore the 'pearl' in a pebble
Once it's been removed
And focus only on those cut and polished
Learning nothing from those lessons not approved

For if it wasn't for broken pebbles
The 'gems' of life would not be true
When the two are placed together
An artwork is formed … a unique and beautiful you!

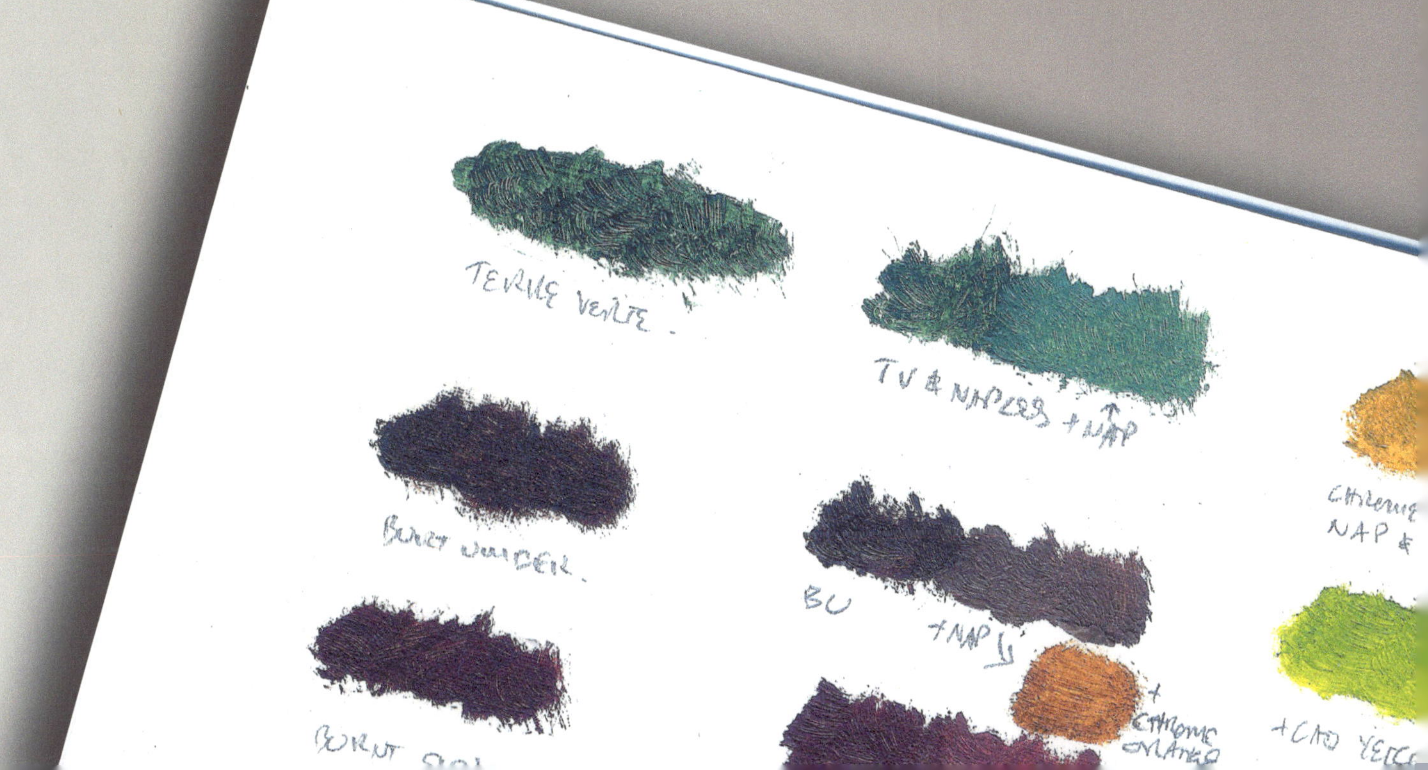

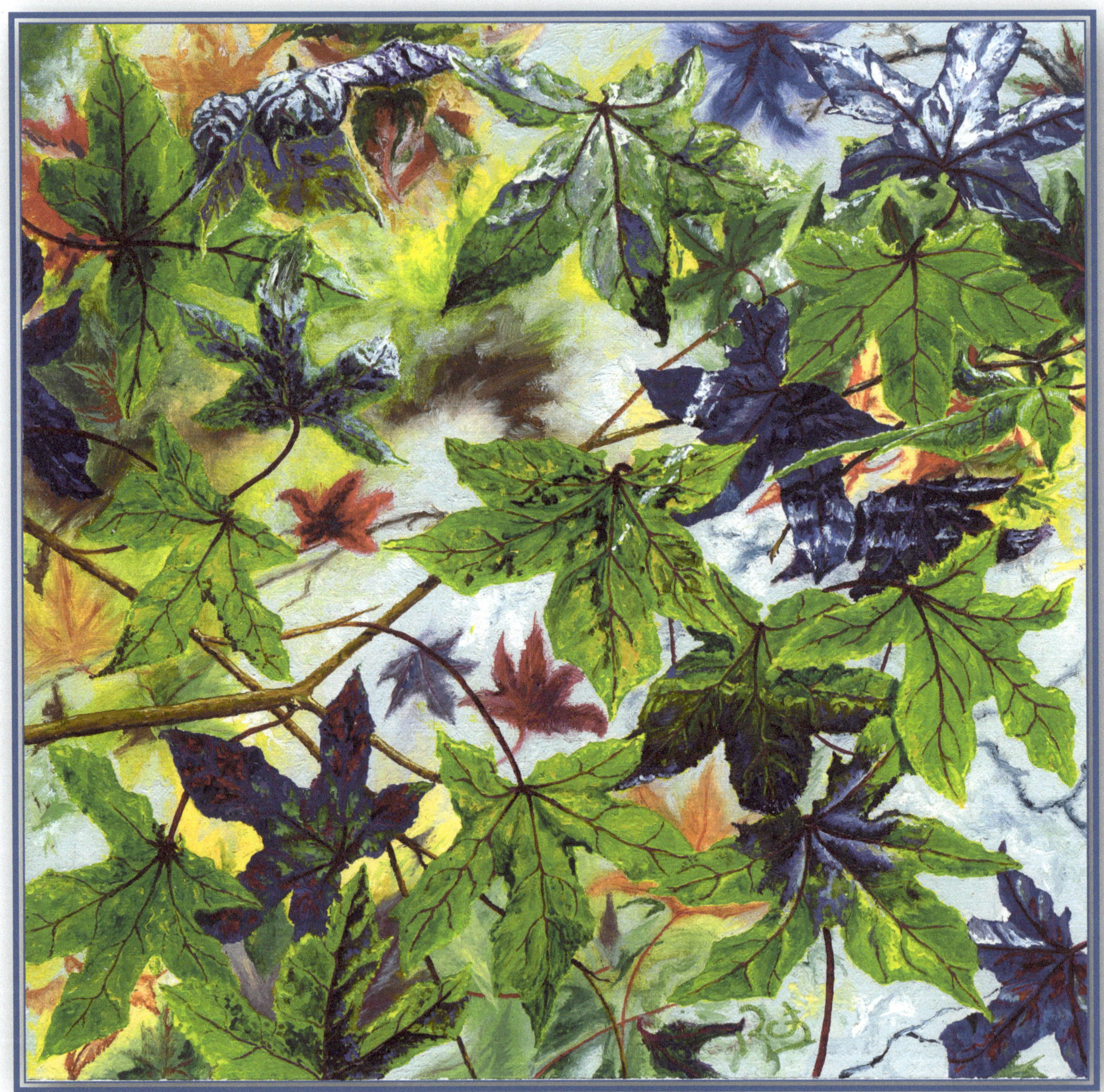

I've Seen …

Late 1992 – Early 1993
I've noticed a woman who stands out from the crowd
She has a shine that seems different from the rest
So how do I get close to her
And will I be allowed?

    Why am I so frightened, to say what's on my chest?
    "Tell the truth in love," I said
    But do I have the courage, do I have the strength?
    It took hours to write two pages in length

As you read my body shook, even though the day was warm
But soon however, my skies turned to grey
For your words "not now" were all that it took
To make my heart fall away and for bitter feelings to swarm

    Because of the hurt you caused inside
    I paid it back with all I could find
    And yet you remained a special friend
    A mystery I struggle to comprehend

'Penny Lover, don't walk on by'
You left me behind, but my love didn't end
With every moment I spent by you
I always found that familiar lie

    For eight painful months
    I was bound like a prisoner
    Controlled by the external hate
    With a conscious act so fake

I mistreated you – yet I still loved?
Though deep inside, my heart cried for you
Crying out to touch, hold and love
All those things I was once afraid to do

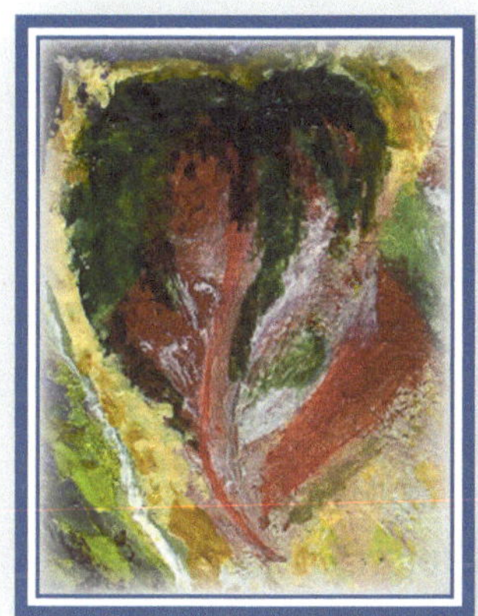

Late 1993
Every moment you were with him
Pain after pain stabbed my heart
I've accepted the fact, 'She's happy Lord'
Though why am I so sad within?

    She says "I'm not suited" but I say I am!
    If it be Your Will Lord?
    Let me have her, take care of her, be mine
    I wish she wasn't so blind

'Take good care of my baby
Be just as kind as you can be
And if you should discover that you don't really love her
Just send my baby back home to me'

Lord if only You would give
As I promise to make her happy
For as long as I shall live

    'Cause I would give anything I own
    Give up my life, my heart, my home
    I would give everything I own
    Just to have you back again'

To Be Continued …

Gemstones

Hydrated organic gemstones
Commonly known as pearls
Are produced within molluscs
Especially those with a two part shell
You consist of two parts
One is a spirit and the other a body
But what if the Holy Spirit
Was asked inside to live and dwell?

      The mollusc uses nacre
      To build its outer home
      But if an object is purposely placed within
      In just the right place
      It will cause the animal to respond
      In a beautiful and creative way
      And at a rate of 1 millimetre per year
      The object is coated in a platelet case

            Platelets build up over time to produce
            The lustre and colour we know as pearl
            Lustre describes the brilliance of inner reflections
            Combined with diffracted light from its outer sphere
            When indwelt by the Holy Spirit
            The light that you shine, is that of Christ
            His lustre splits into an array of colours
            Casting a glow to all who come near

                  The radiance of a pearl
                  Is the light that is reflected
                  Not just off the surface
                  But through all the layers within
                  Deeper lustre and brighter radiance
                  Are achieved when the nacre crystals
                  Covering the object are uniform
                  And the layers are numerous and thin

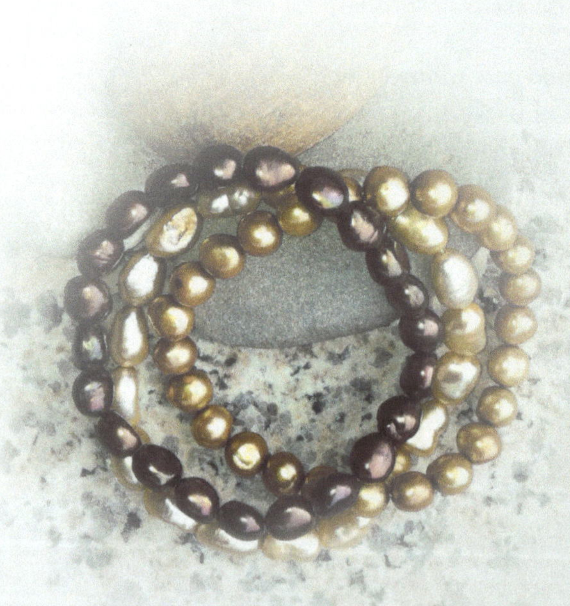

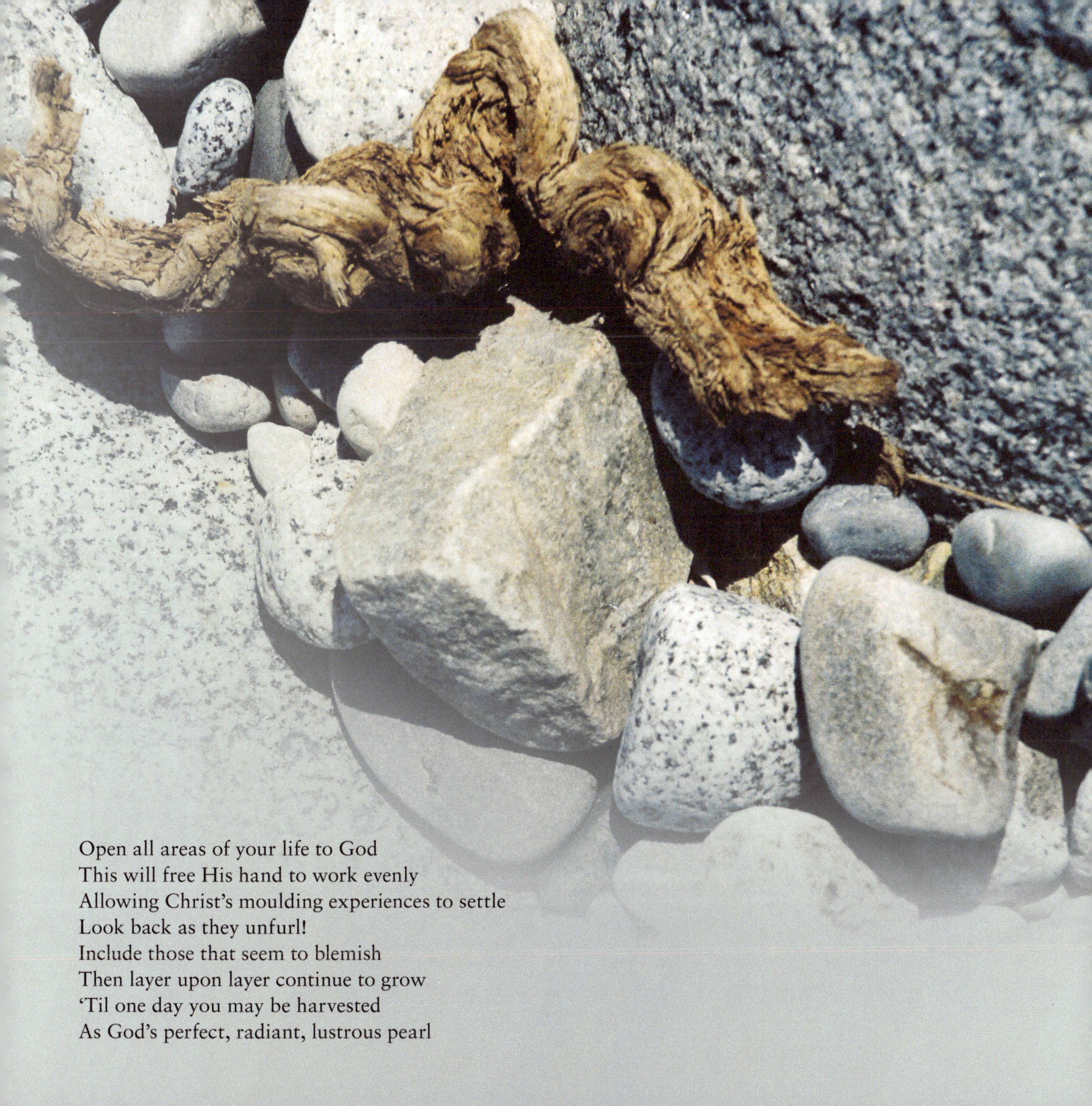
Open all areas of your life to God
This will free His hand to work evenly
Allowing Christ's moulding experiences to settle
Look back as they unfurl!
Include those that seem to blemish
Then layer upon layer continue to grow
'Til one day you may be harvested
As God's perfect, radiant, lustrous pearl

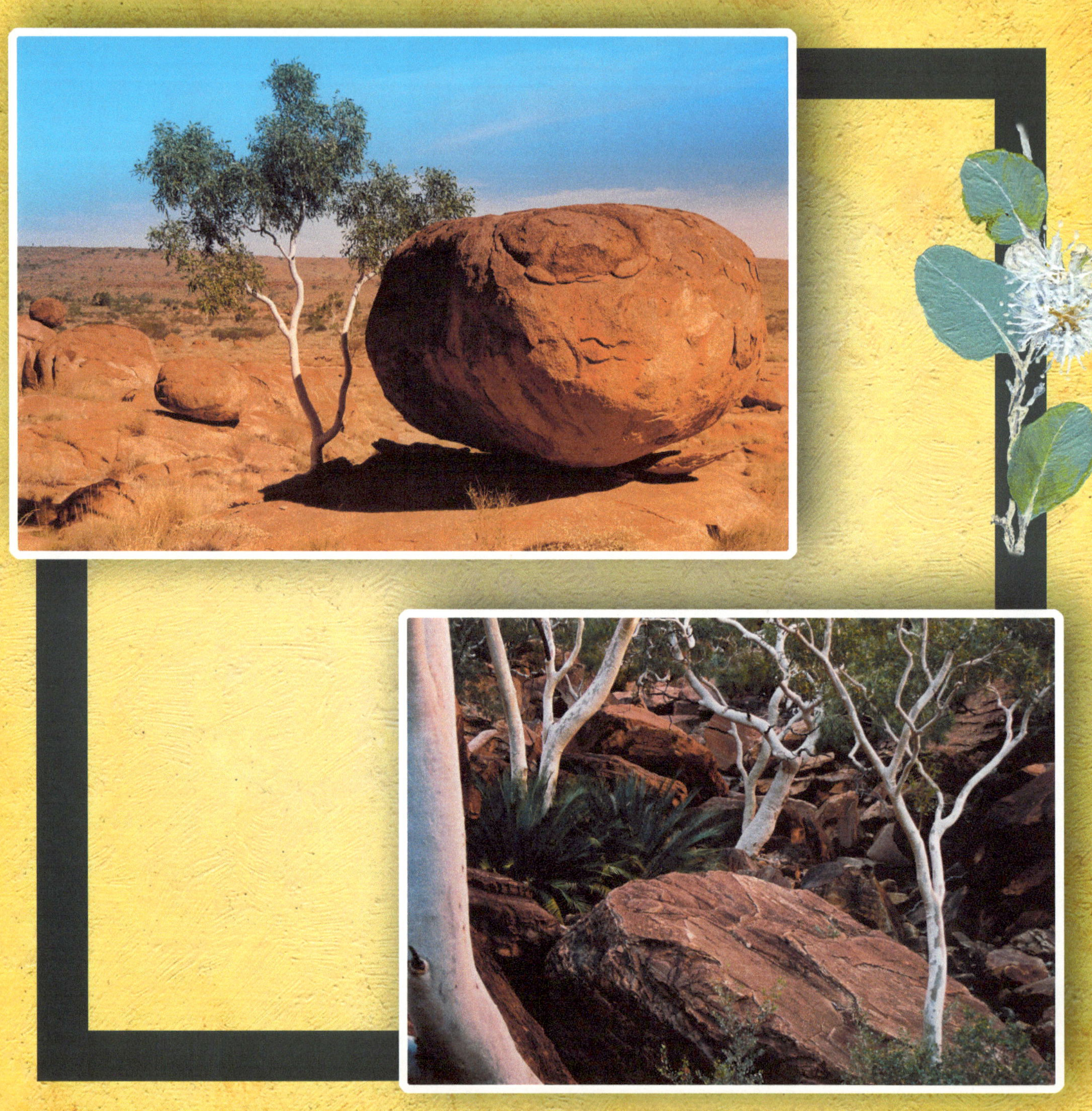

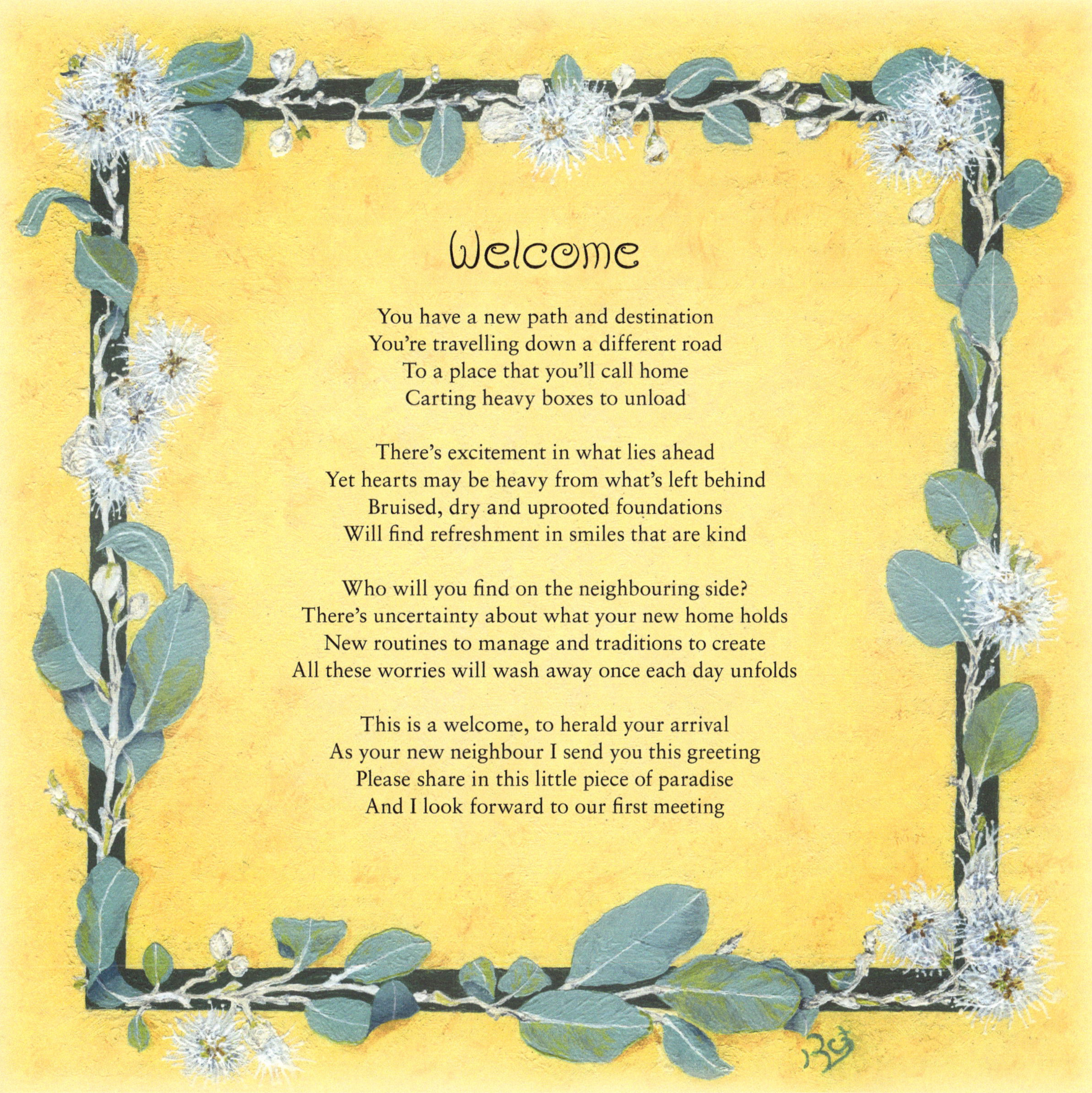

Welcome

You have a new path and destination
You're travelling down a different road
To a place that you'll call home
Carting heavy boxes to unload

There's excitement in what lies ahead
Yet hearts may be heavy from what's left behind
Bruised, dry and uprooted foundations
Will find refreshment in smiles that are kind

Who will you find on the neighbouring side?
There's uncertainty about what your new home holds
New routines to manage and traditions to create
All these worries will wash away once each day unfolds

This is a welcome, to herald your arrival
As your new neighbour I send you this greeting
Please share in this little piece of paradise
And I look forward to our first meeting

Jealous Love

<u>Research</u>

Piercing the pearl of wisdom, to find the fourth dimension
Is a practice called yoga, to increase one's awareness through inner observation

Yoga is a meditation of self-discovery, training each individual part
To recede deeper to the atman, in a disciplinary art

Through the act of controlling and blocking, the thoughts of and from the mind
It enables the yogi to feel relaxed, at peace and then perfect happiness they will find

The true self manifests outward, through latent deep sleep and active dreaming
Into the waking city of the body, united to the conscious mind by breathing

The senses and actions from the body, are then a direct projection from the soul
Heaven is the heart of a being, God is the true self, in the centre of the whole

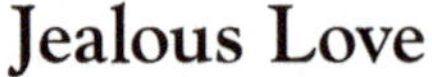

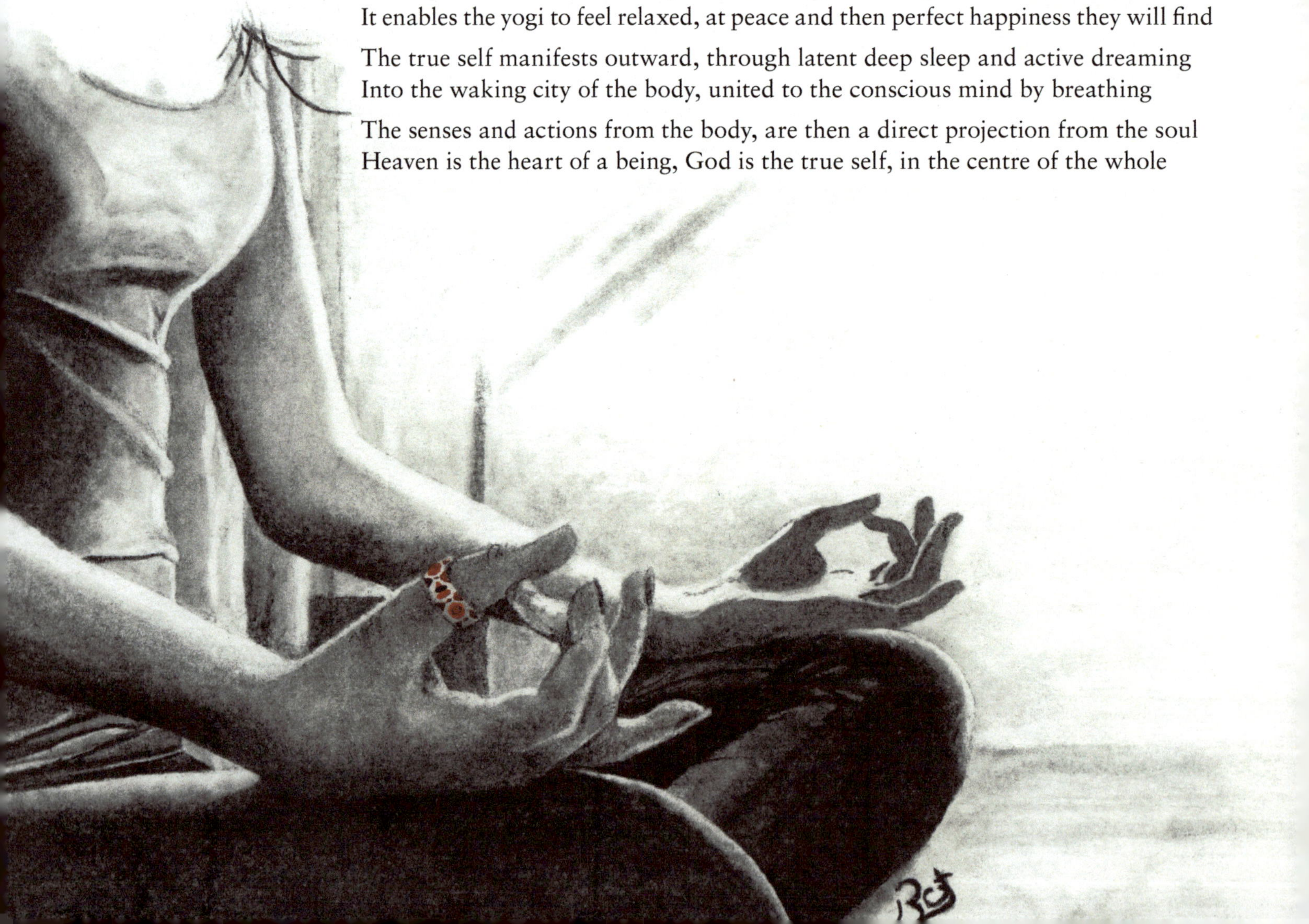

There arise some thoughts I have, that must face a yogi in their quest
To attain a pure blissful state, or perfect peace and inner happiness

If the outer self is imperfect, then so must be the inner centre
Therefore yoga must be practiced daily. The effects don't last forever

If the following is true, about perfection and the state of purity
It cannot come from imperfection, even once I've found my ultimate reality

So when I pierce the pearl of wisdom, will it only leave me jealous of the illusion
When the mind's centre beneath the layers, is merely the source of my imperfection?

When I return to waking relaxed and peaceful, what will be waiting?
Guilt or worry for the future, and pain from the past still enduring?

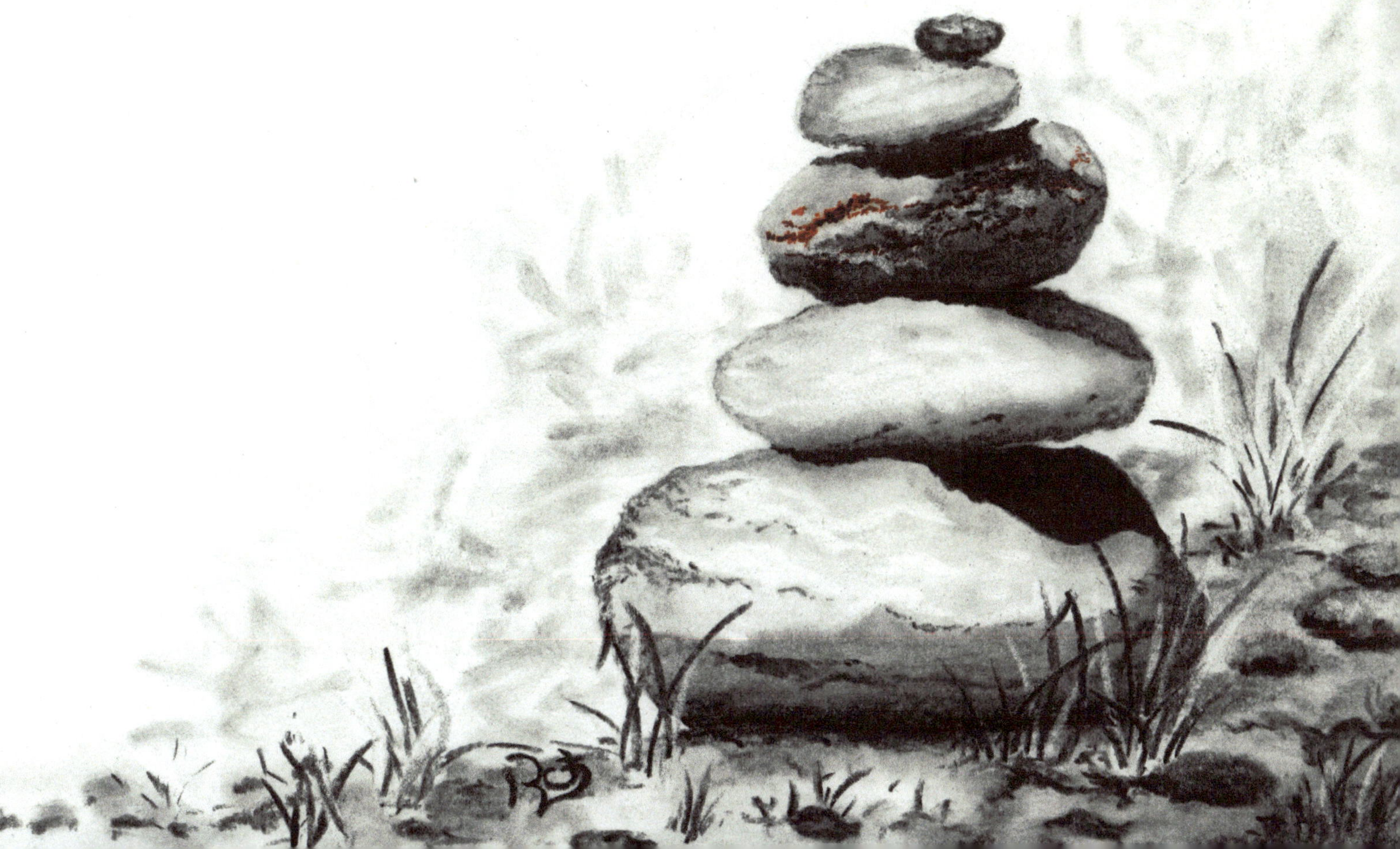

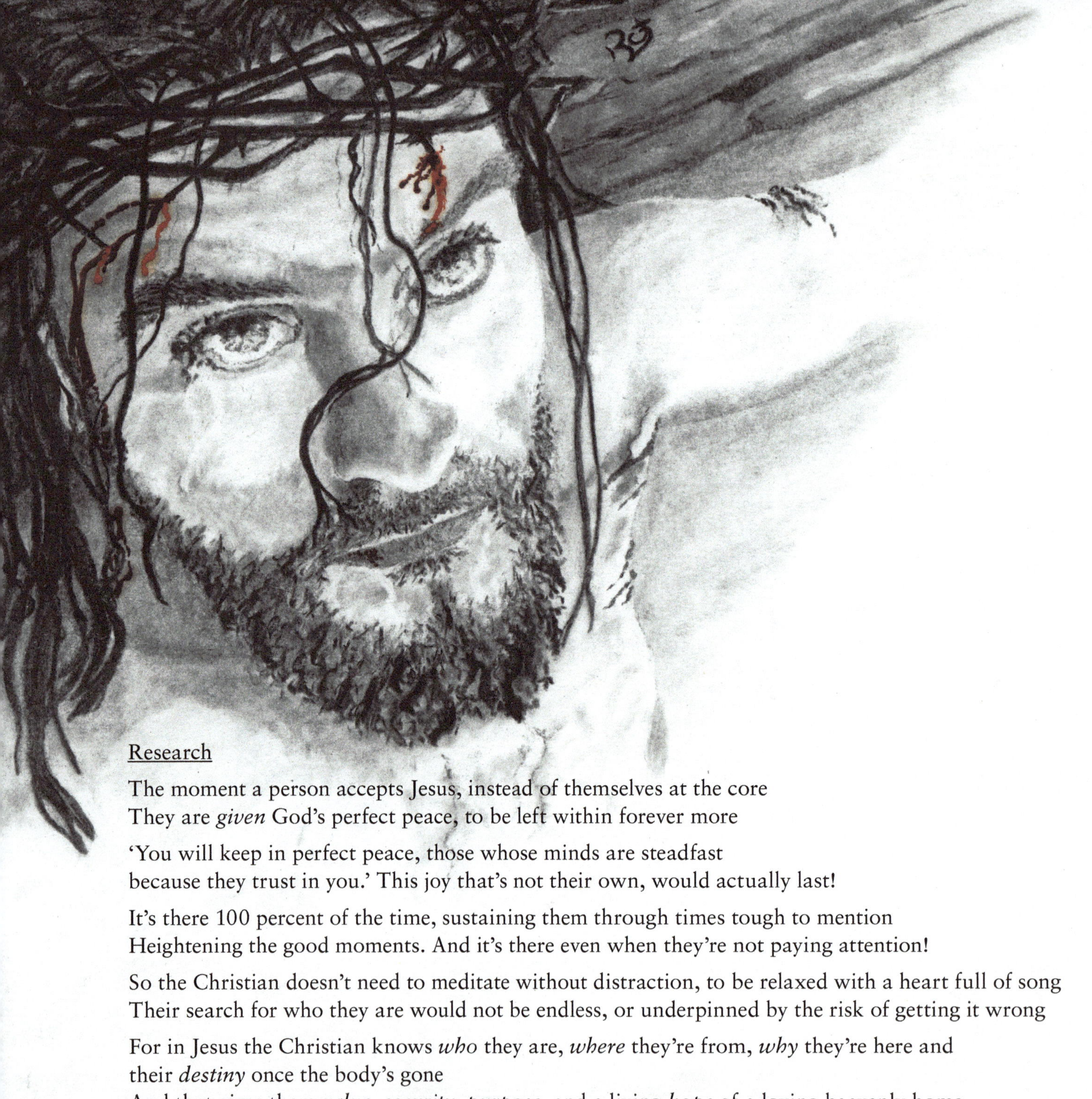

Research

The moment a person accepts Jesus, instead of themselves at the core
They are *given* God's perfect peace, to be left within forever more

'You will keep in perfect peace, those whose minds are steadfast
because they trust in you.' This joy that's not their own, would actually last!

It's there 100 percent of the time, sustaining them through times tough to mention
Heightening the good moments. And it's there even when they're not paying attention!

So the Christian doesn't need to meditate without distraction, to be relaxed with a heart full of song
Their search for who they are would not be endless, or underpinned by the risk of getting it wrong

For in Jesus the Christian knows *who* they are, *where* they're from, *why* they're here and
their *destiny* once the body's gone
And that gives them *value*, *security*, *purpose*, and a living *hope* of a loving heavenly home

<u>Personal Reflections</u>

Many names have been given, about the Divine Being described in the Biblical Word
Though the name of 'Jealous', I've not often heard

God loves too much to share me with another, with my true self or even just with me
Christians are also jealous for me, with longing hearts to shine the 'Truth' that they see

The Lord states He sees my future complete. Because He's in control, I need not worry
Any pain of my past He's able to heal, previous wrongs are forgiven and forgotten with just a "sorry"

Though I have not seen Him, He cries "be not afraid to believe and love,"
And then be filled beyond measure, with an inexpressible and glorious joy from above

And the peace of God, which transcends all my understanding
Will guard my heart and mind in Jesus, whose mercy graces every given blessing

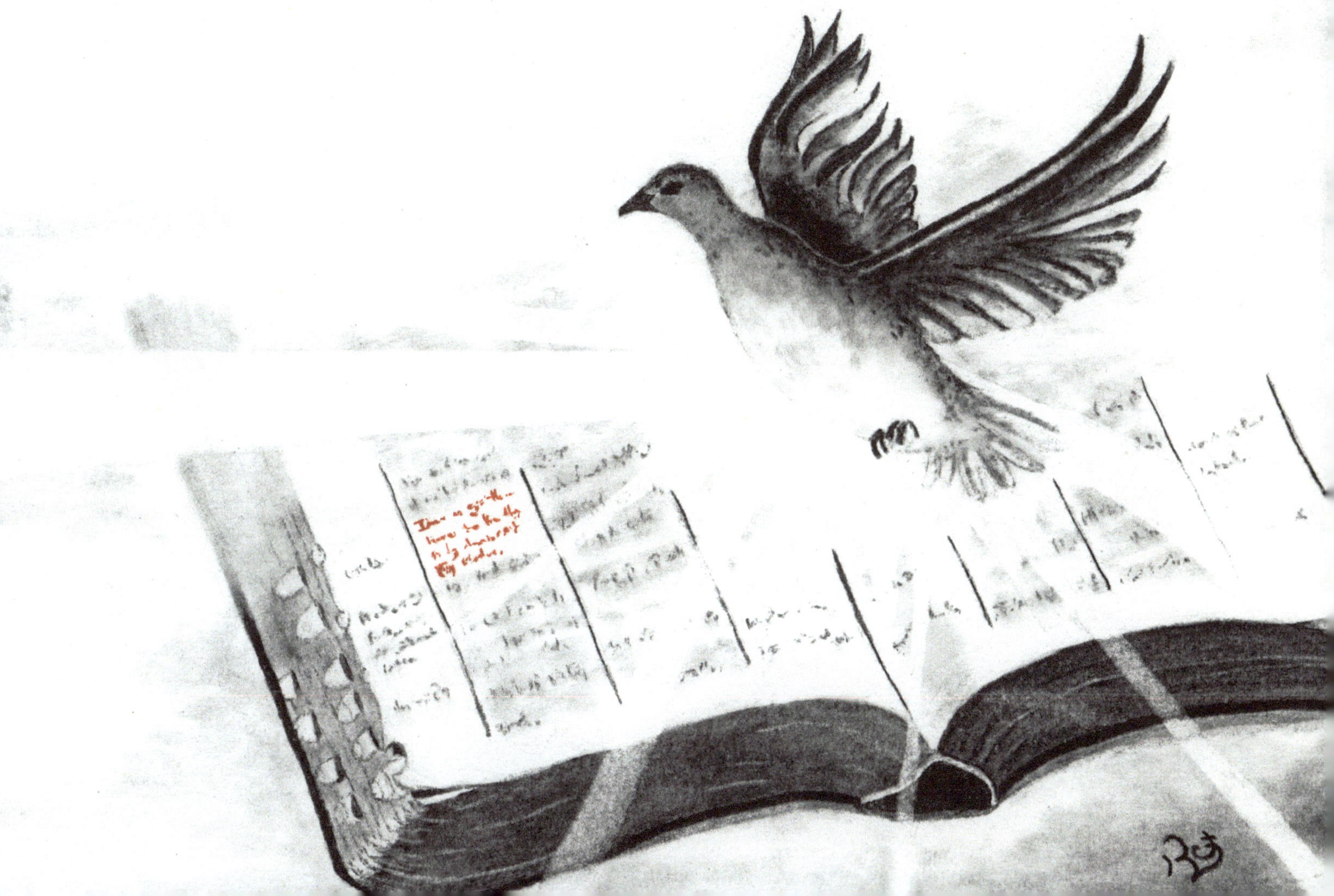

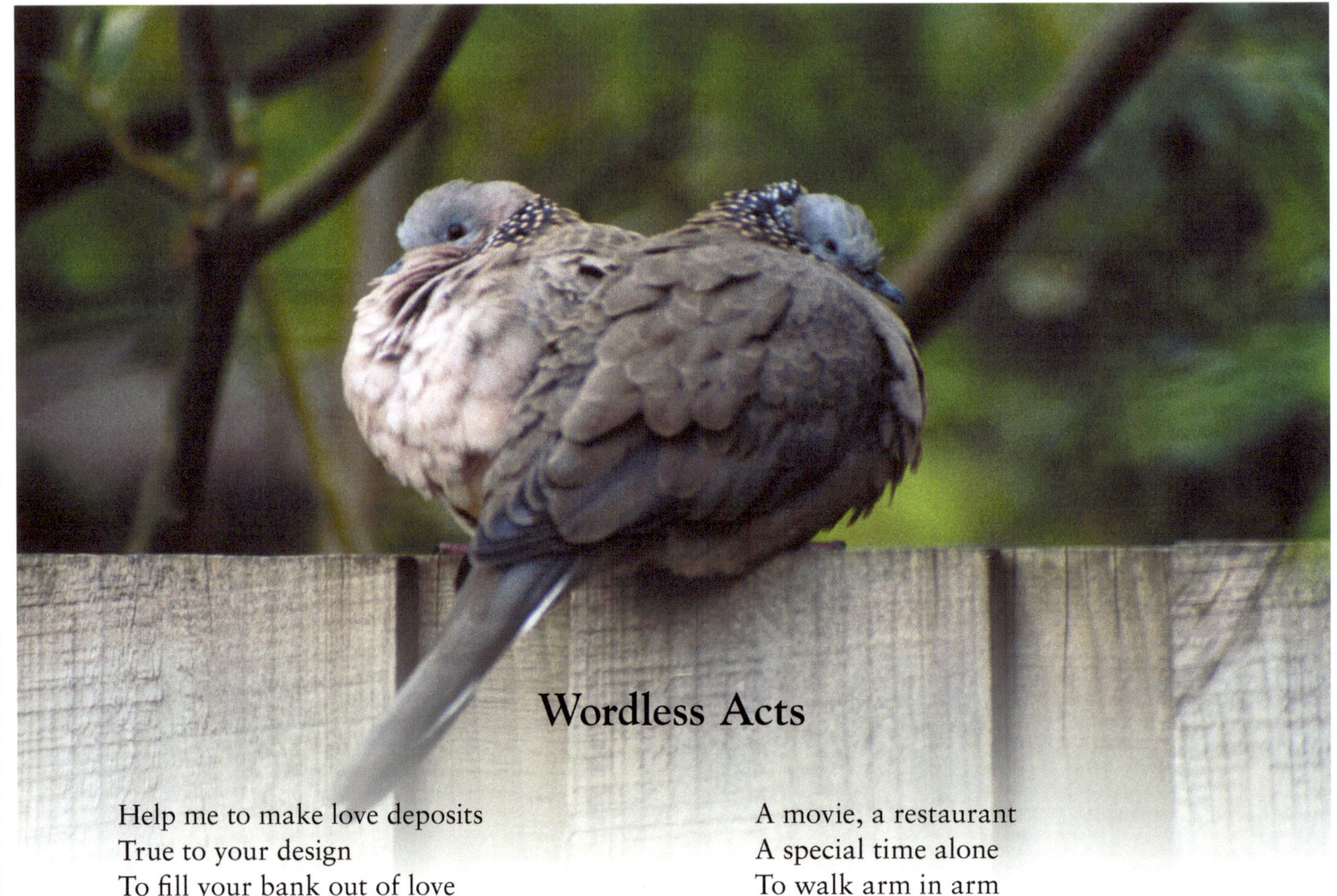

Wordless Acts

Help me to make love deposits
True to your design
To fill your bank out of love
And not compelled by wanting mine

To offer love as a gift
Not as an act of manipulation
Designed to curb your mood or make you happy
That is far from God's creation

An act to sense again
That tender touch so kind
A cherishing look or an act of compassion
Which I seldom feel outside a sexual time

A movie, a restaurant
A special time alone
To walk arm in arm
Through memories that have not gone

Help me to make deposits
To say what I feel with wordless acts
To express in your language
What your heart often lacks

I Love You

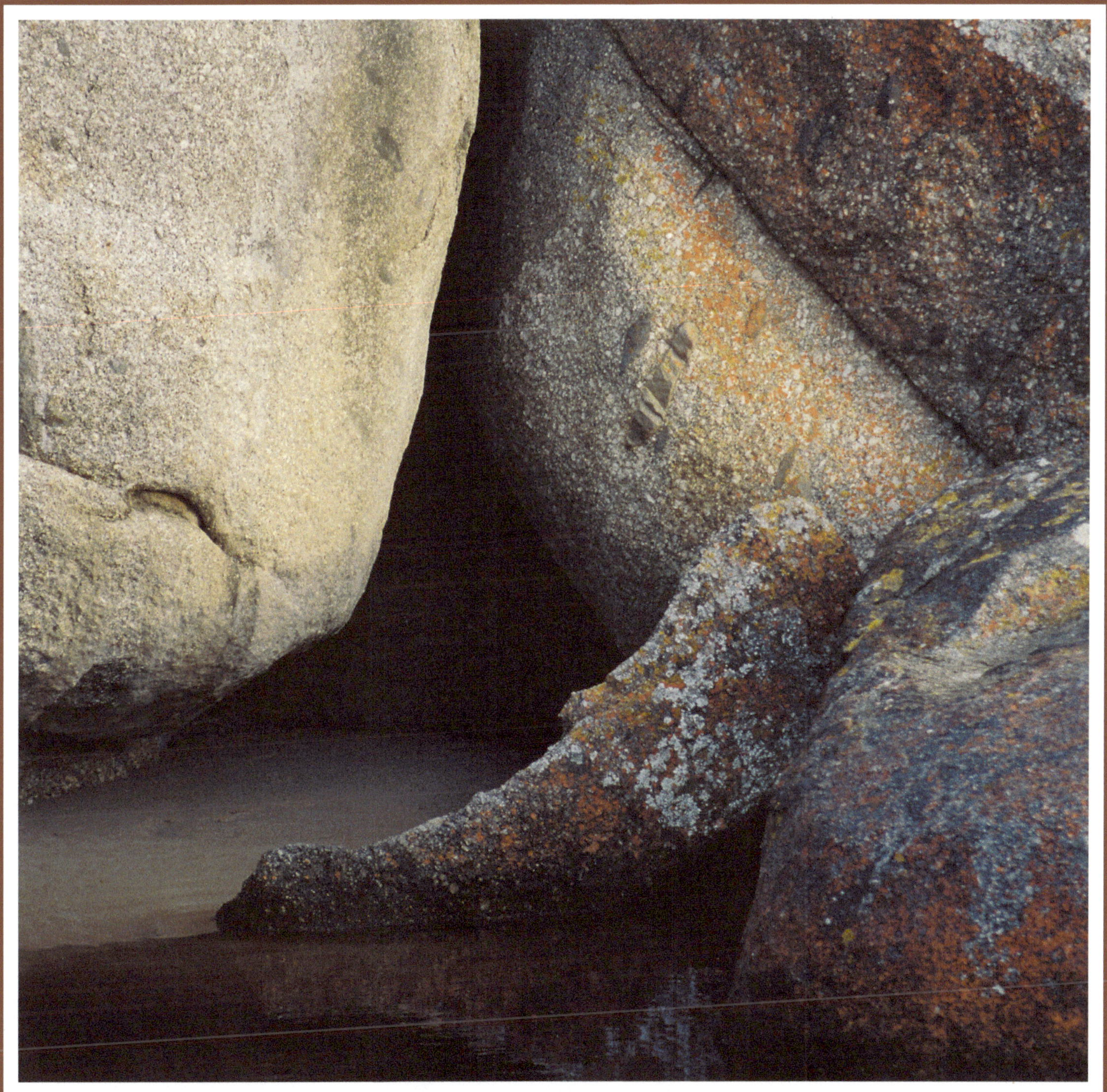

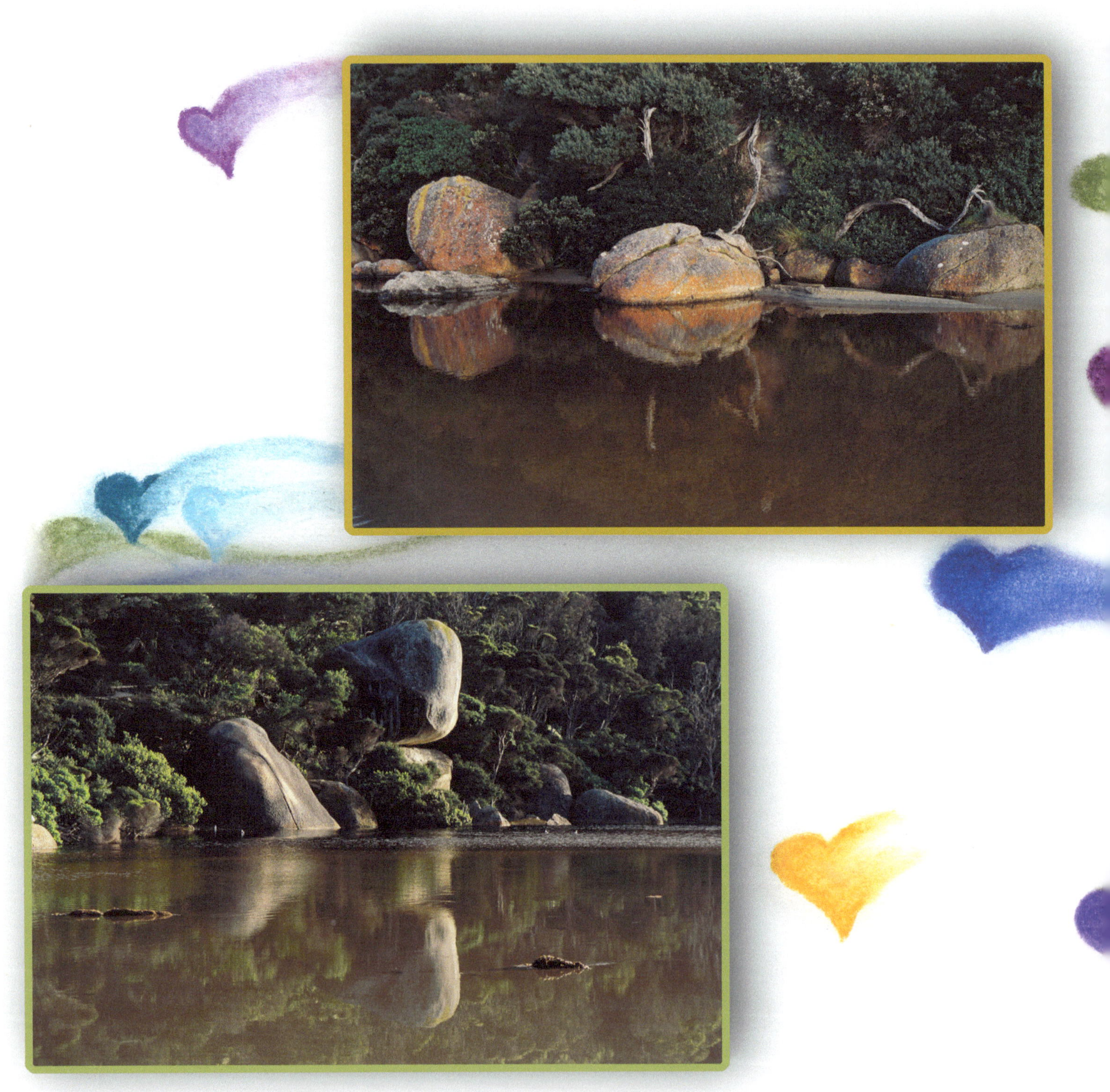

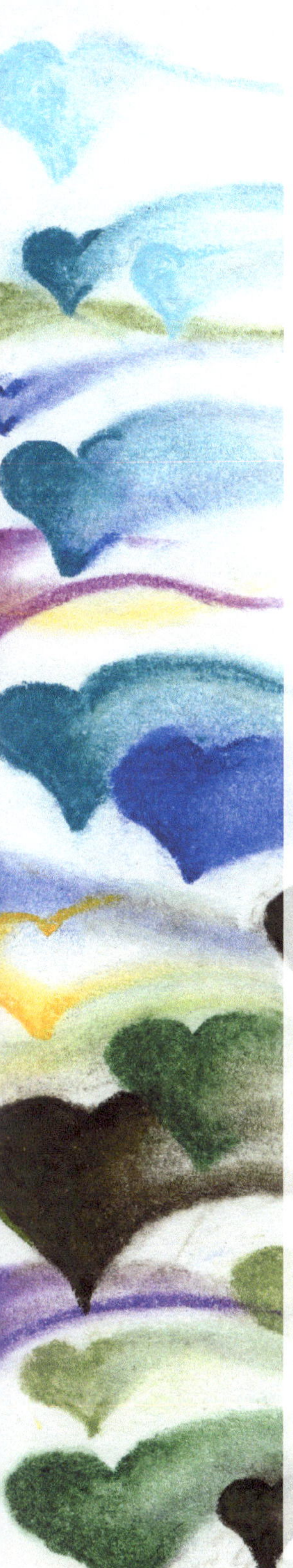

God the Father

From: God <godthefather@heaven.son>
Sent: Now
To: mychild@earthlyfamily.kin
Subject: Freedom

Dear Child,

Who are you?
If they took away your name
If your birth certificate was burnt
Would you be the same?

Have you found meaning and fulfilment
In the job you do or seek?
Or, is there complete satisfaction
In the pastimes that you keep?

Can you define the void deep within yourself?
Do you feel you're a pointless existence?
Are you searching for your life's true purpose
That can really make a difference?

Where is that elusive perfect love
Passing by in dreams as you have slept?
Have you seen it in family or friends
Or in past relationships you have kept?

As a unique child of mine
Through my Son, I wish to adopt you
Accepting you unconditionally, as you are
Your past forgotten and your life refreshed anew

A tailor made purpose has been set
To make a difference to the world, with a life really worth living
To give you meaning and fulfilment
There is more to your life than just existing

I am not your condemning Judge
Contrary to what is said about Me
My love for you is perfect, unchanging, unfailing
I ache to be a friend and to set you completely... *free*

... Love

God The Father

Address: Eternity Way, HEAVEN 777
Phone: 1777PRAYER
Email: godthefather@heaven.son

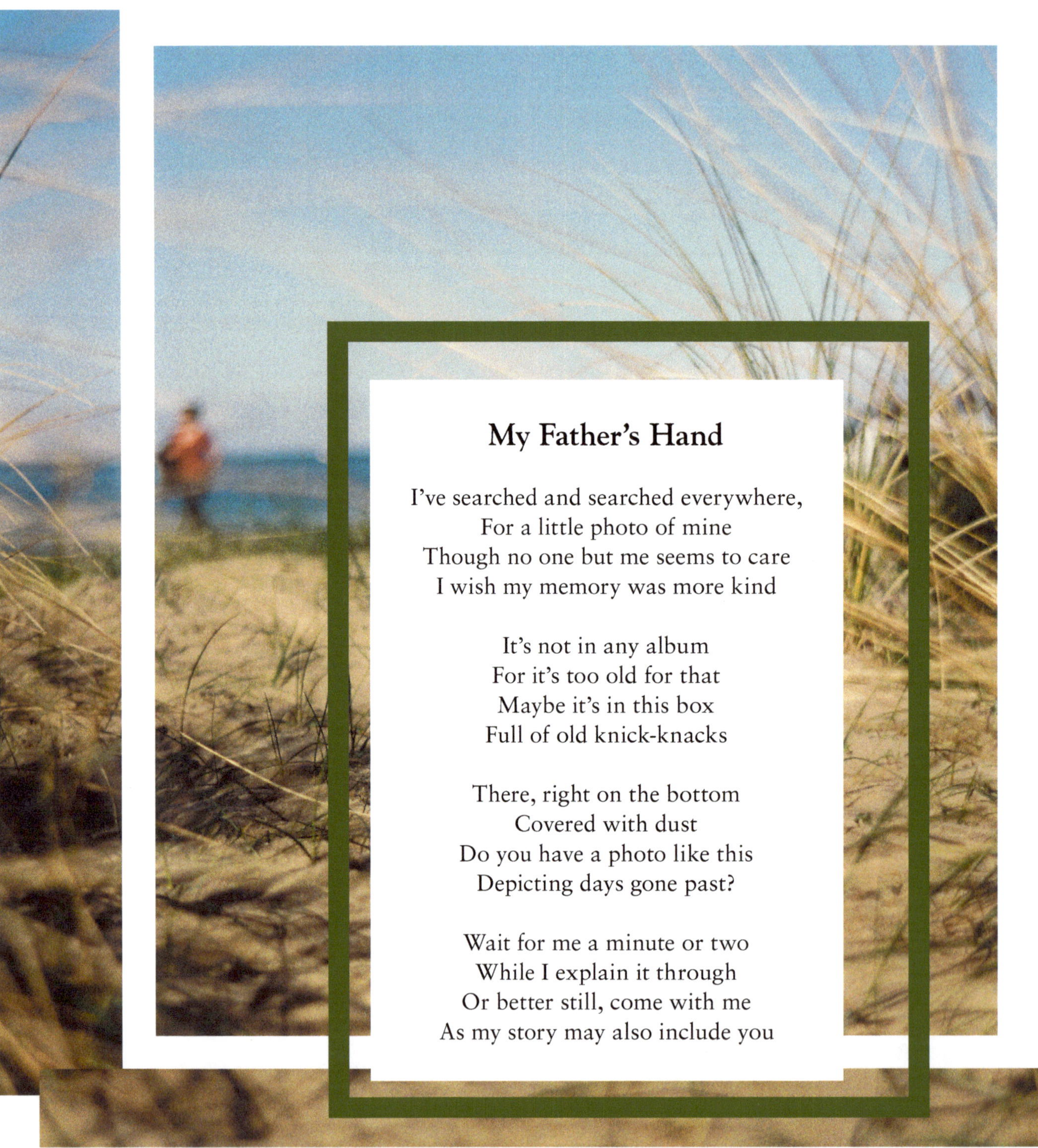

My Father's Hand

I've searched and searched everywhere,
For a little photo of mine
Though no one but me seems to care
I wish my memory was more kind

It's not in any album
For it's too old for that
Maybe it's in this box
Full of old knick-knacks

There, right on the bottom
Covered with dust
Do you have a photo like this
Depicting days gone past?

Wait for me a minute or two
While I explain it through
Or better still, come with me
As my story may also include you

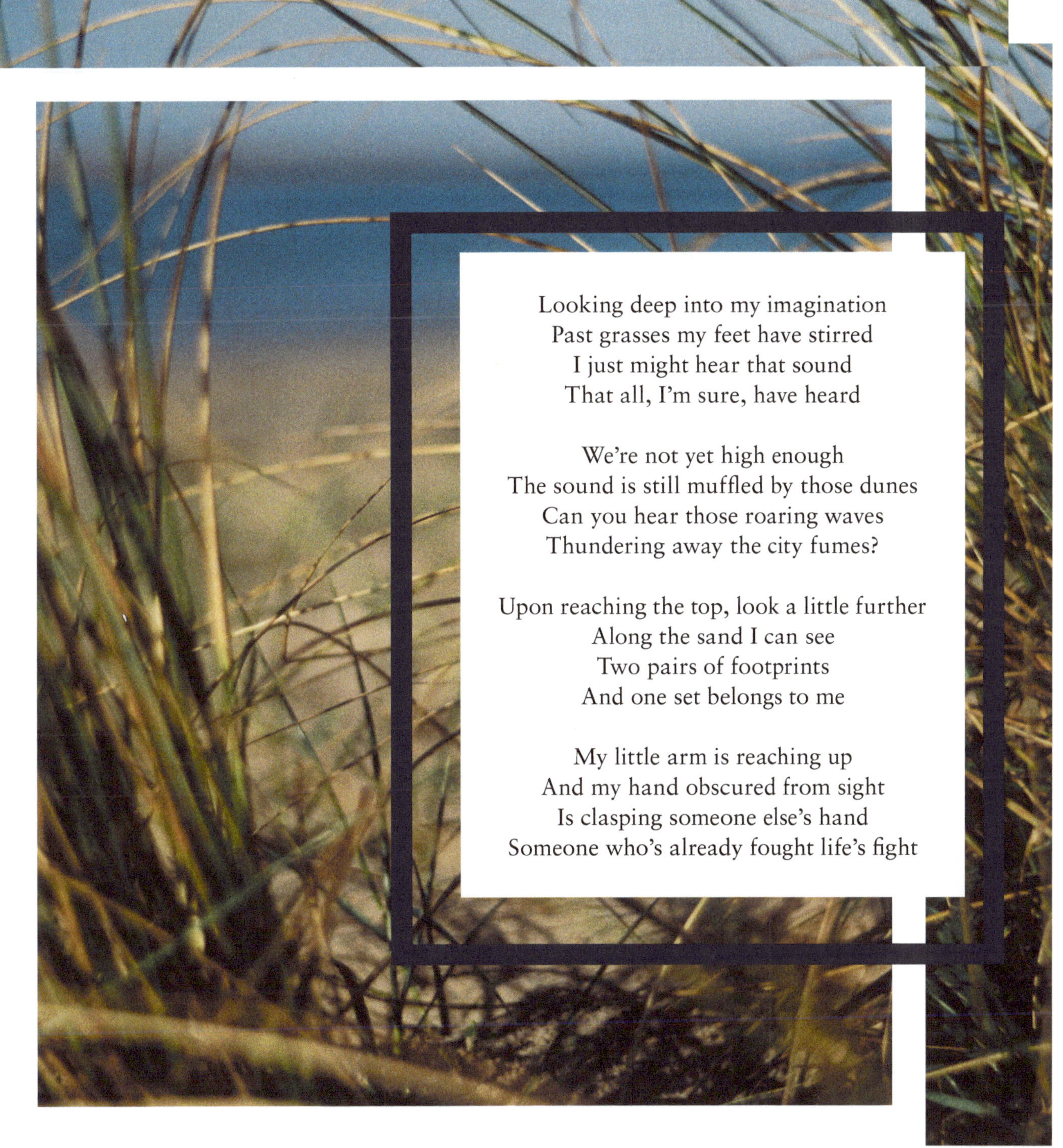

Looking deep into my imagination
Past grasses my feet have stirred
I just might hear that sound
That all, I'm sure, have heard

We're not yet high enough
The sound is still muffled by those dunes
Can you hear those roaring waves
Thundering away the city fumes?

Upon reaching the top, look a little further
Along the sand I can see
Two pairs of footprints
And one set belongs to me

My little arm is reaching up
And my hand obscured from sight
Is clasping someone else's hand
Someone who's already fought life's fight

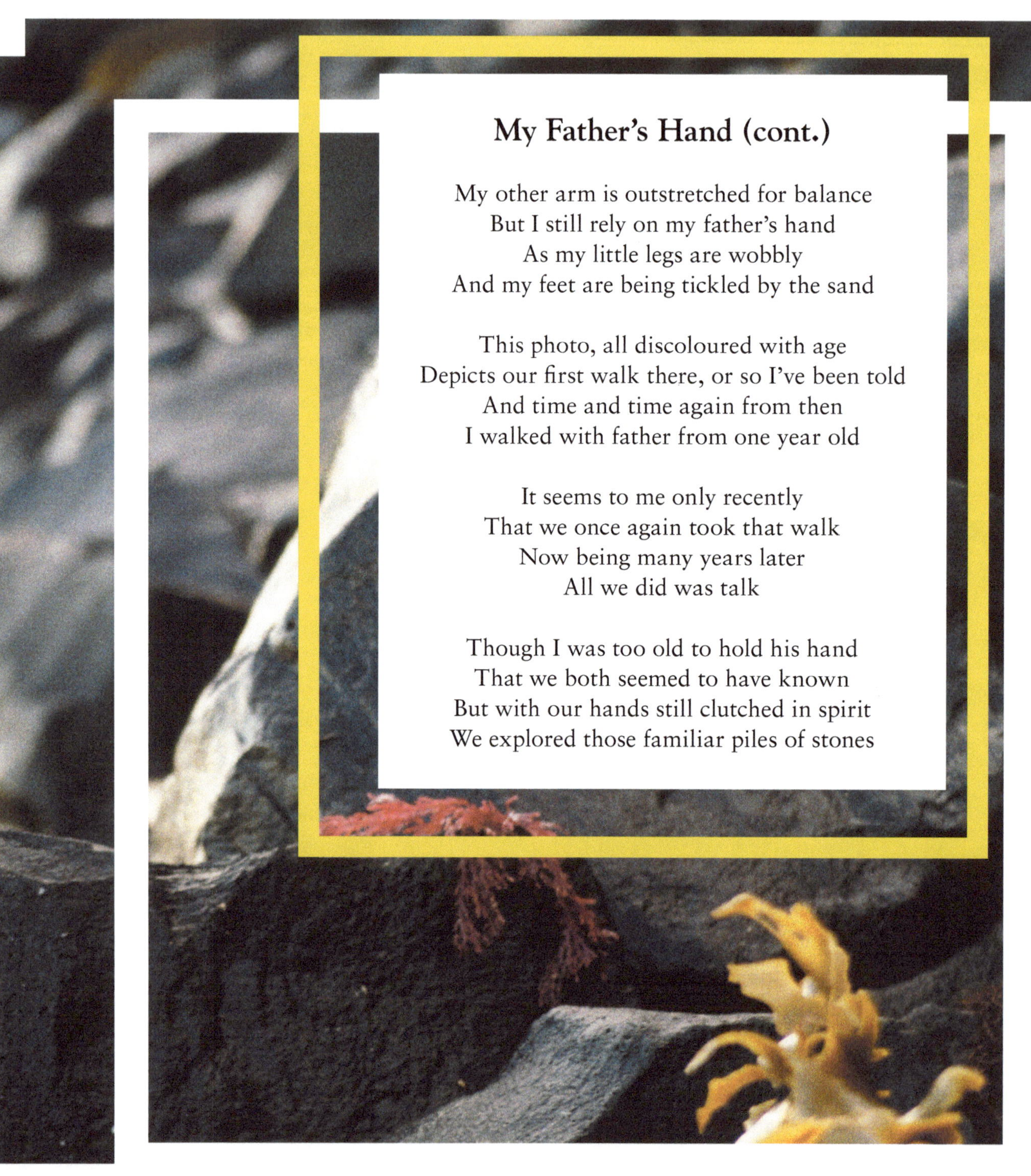

My Father's Hand (cont.)

My other arm is outstretched for balance
But I still rely on my father's hand
As my little legs are wobbly
And my feet are being tickled by the sand

This photo, all discoloured with age
Depicts our first walk there, or so I've been told
And time and time again from then
I walked with father from one year old

It seems to me only recently
That we once again took that walk
Now being many years later
All we did was talk

Though I was too old to hold his hand
That we both seemed to have known
But with our hands still clutched in spirit
We explored those familiar piles of stones

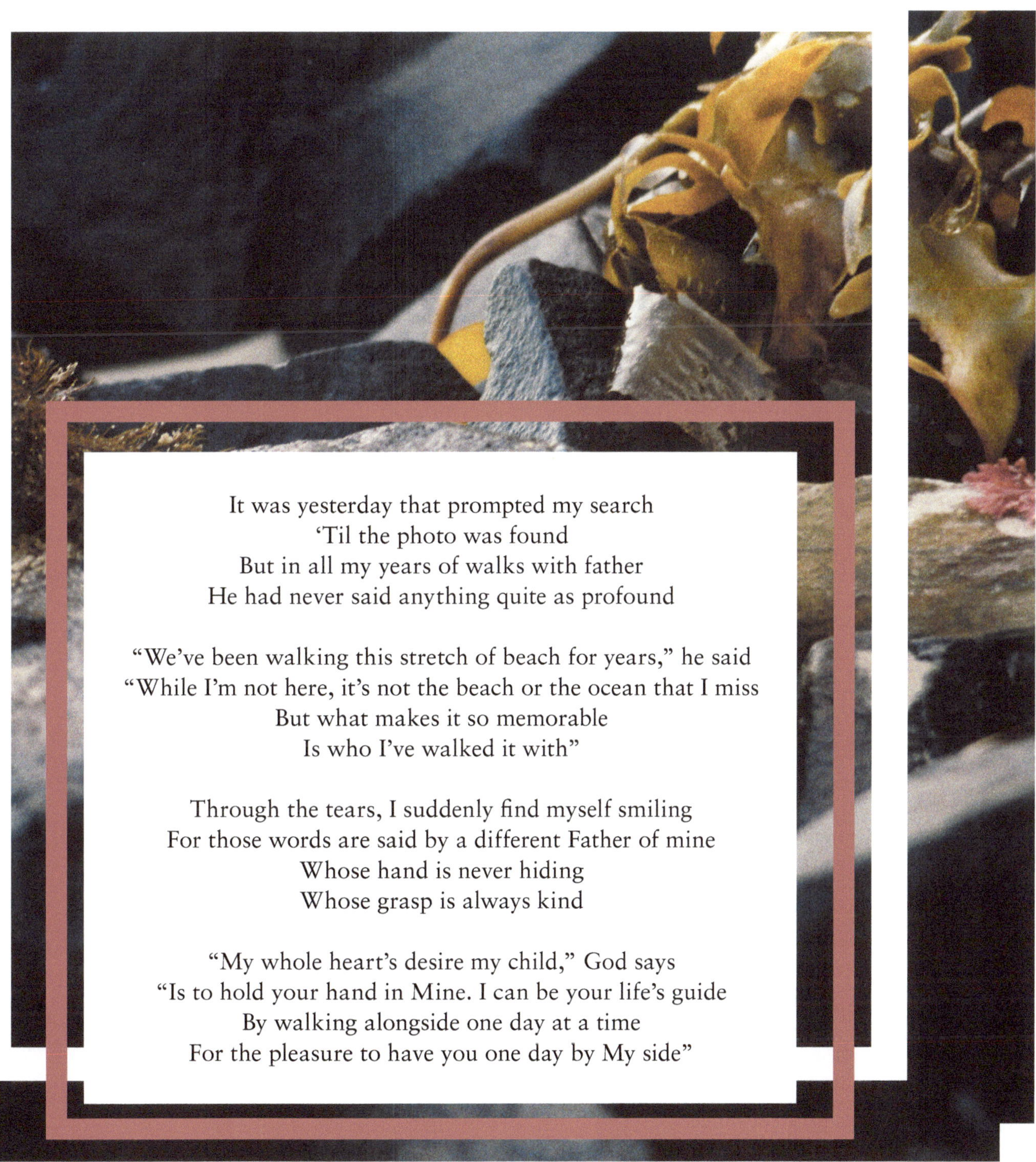

It was yesterday that prompted my search
'Til the photo was found
But in all my years of walks with father
He had never said anything quite as profound

"We've been walking this stretch of beach for years," he said
"While I'm not here, it's not the beach or the ocean that I miss
But what makes it so memorable
Is who I've walked it with"

Through the tears, I suddenly find myself smiling
For those words are said by a different Father of mine
Whose hand is never hiding
Whose grasp is always kind

"My whole heart's desire my child," God says
"Is to hold your hand in Mine. I can be your life's guide
By walking alongside one day at a time
For the pleasure to have you one day by My side"

<u>References</u>

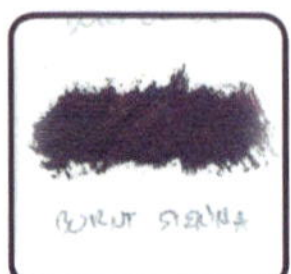

Forepoem :   Penned 11th June 2011
Reference :   Ezekiel 36:27 (MSG)

'I'll put my Spirit in you and make it possible for you to do what I tell you and live by my commands.'

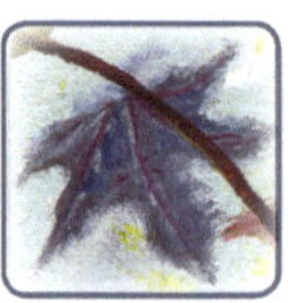

I've Seen … Part 1 :   Complete Poem Penned for 27th June 1994
Oil Painting :   Named 'Passing – Part 1' Oct 2012 : 'Liquidambar' or 'American Sweetgum'
                             (*Liquidambar styraciflua*)
Notes :   Written from a man's perspective – To Be Continued
Reference :   Ephesians 4:15 (NIV)

'Instead, speaking the truth in love, we will grow to become in every respect the mature body of him who is the head, that is, Christ.'

Acknowledgements :   'Penny Lover' Lionel Richie 1992
                             'Take Good Care of My Baby' Bobby Vee 1961
                             'Everything I Own' Bread 1972

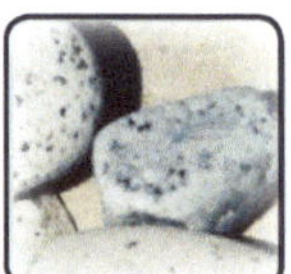

Gemstones :   Penned for the 4th February 2009
Photograph :   'Blue Stone Bay', Freycinet National Park, Tasmania, Australia
Notes :   Is it a Pebble or a Pearl?
Reference :   Romans 5:3-5 (MSG)

'There's more to come: We continue to shout our praise even when we're hemmed in with troubles, because we know how troubles can develop passionate patience in us, and how that patience in turn forges the tempered steel of virtue, keeping us alert for whatever God will do next. In alert expectancy such as this, we're never left feeling short changed. Quite the contrary – we can't round up enough containers to hold everything God generously pours into our lives through the Holy Spirit!'

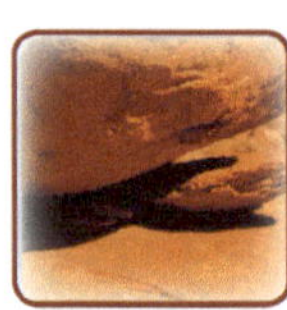

Photograph :
 'Devils Marbles',
 Karlu Karlu Conservation Reserve,
 Northern Territory, Australia

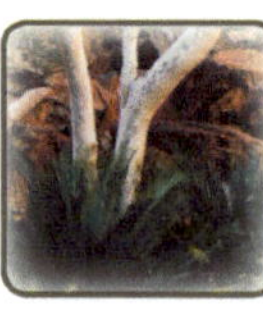

Photograph :
 'Kings Canyon',
 West MacDonnell Ranges,
 Northern Territory, Australia

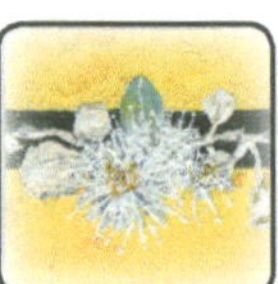

Welcome :   Penned 10th March 2011
Oil Painting :   'White Marlock' (*Eucalyptus Tetragona*)
Reference :   Romans 15:2 (MSG)

'Strength is for service, not status. Each one of us needs to look after the good of the people around us, asking ourselves, "How can I help?"'

<u>References</u>

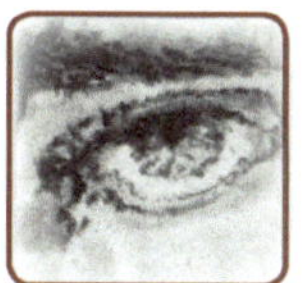

Jealous Love : Penned 15th May 2011 – Rewritten 23rd May 2013
Charcoal Sticks & Oil : Named (in order) 'Struggles?' 'Subject?' 'Salvation?' 'Sharing' Jul 2012:
Depictions of –
   A meditative pose & Zen Stones
   Jesus Christ on the cross & Light/Holy Spirit coming out of the Bible
Reference : Matthew 10:39 (MSG) & Isaiah 45:5-6 (NIV)
(Also 2 Corinthians 11:2a, Isaiah 26:3, John 14:27, Philippians 4:7 & Exodus 34:14 NIV)

'If your first concern is to look after yourself, you'll never find yourself. But if you forget about yourself and look to me, you'll find both yourself and me.'

'I am the LORD, and there is no other; apart from me there is no God. I will strengthen you, though you have not acknowledged me, so that from the rising of the sun to the place of its setting people may know there is none besides me. I am the LORD, and there is no other.'

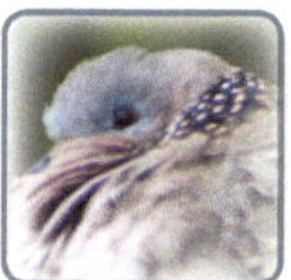

Wordless Acts : Penned 26th July 2007
Photograph : 'Spotted Dove' (*Streptopelia chinensis*)
Reference : Song Of Songs 1:15-16 (MSG)

The Man : 15 'Oh, my dear friend! You're so beautiful! And your eyes so beautiful – like doves!'
The Woman : 16 'And you, my dear lover – you're so handsome! And the bed we share is like a forest glen.'

Dear Child : Penned 20th December 2005
Water Pastel : Named 'God's Emails' Aug 2012
Reference : John 1:12-13 (NIV)

'Yet to all who did receive him, to those who believed in his name, he gave the right to become children of God – children born not of natural descent, nor of human decision or a husband's will, but born of God.'

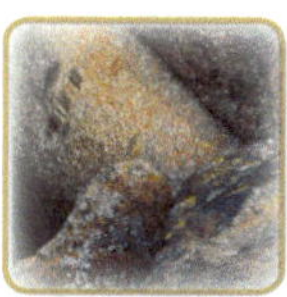

Photograph :
   Granite boulder formation & lichen,
   Wilsons Promontory National Park,
   Gippsland, Victoria, Australia

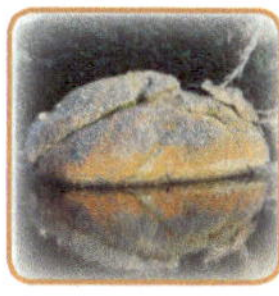

Photograph :
   'Tidal River' scenes,
   Wilsons Promontory National Park,
   Gippsland, Victoria, Australia

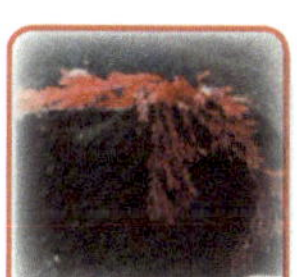

My Fathers Hand : Penned 24th February 2004
Photograph : Beach scenes from 'Barwon Heads', Victoria, Australia
Volcanic Rock & Seaweed, 'Inverloch', Victoria, Australia
Reference : Psalm 139:9-10 (NIV)
'If I rise on the wings of the dawn, if I settle on the far side of the sea, even there your hand will guide me, your right hand will hold me fast.'

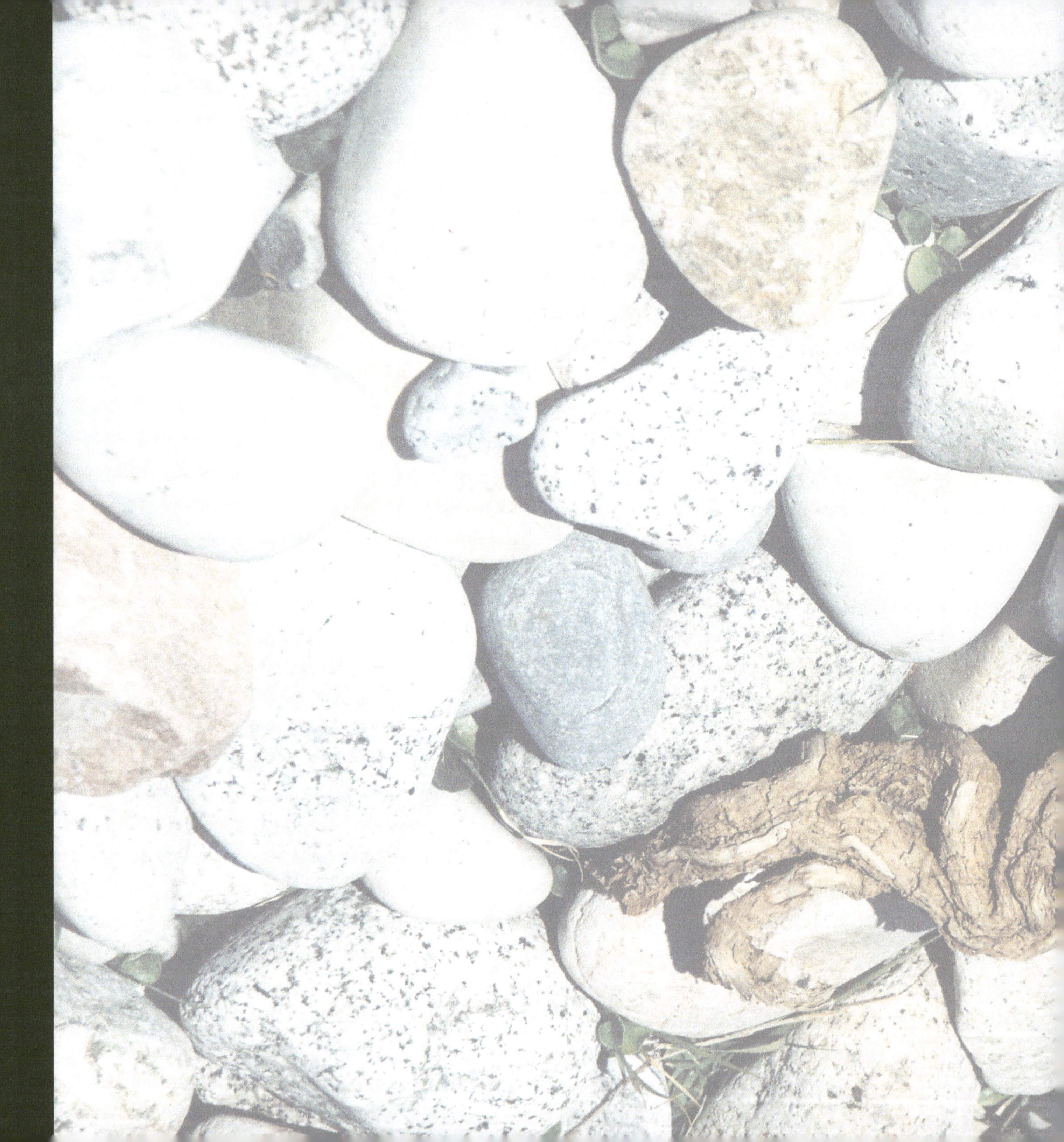

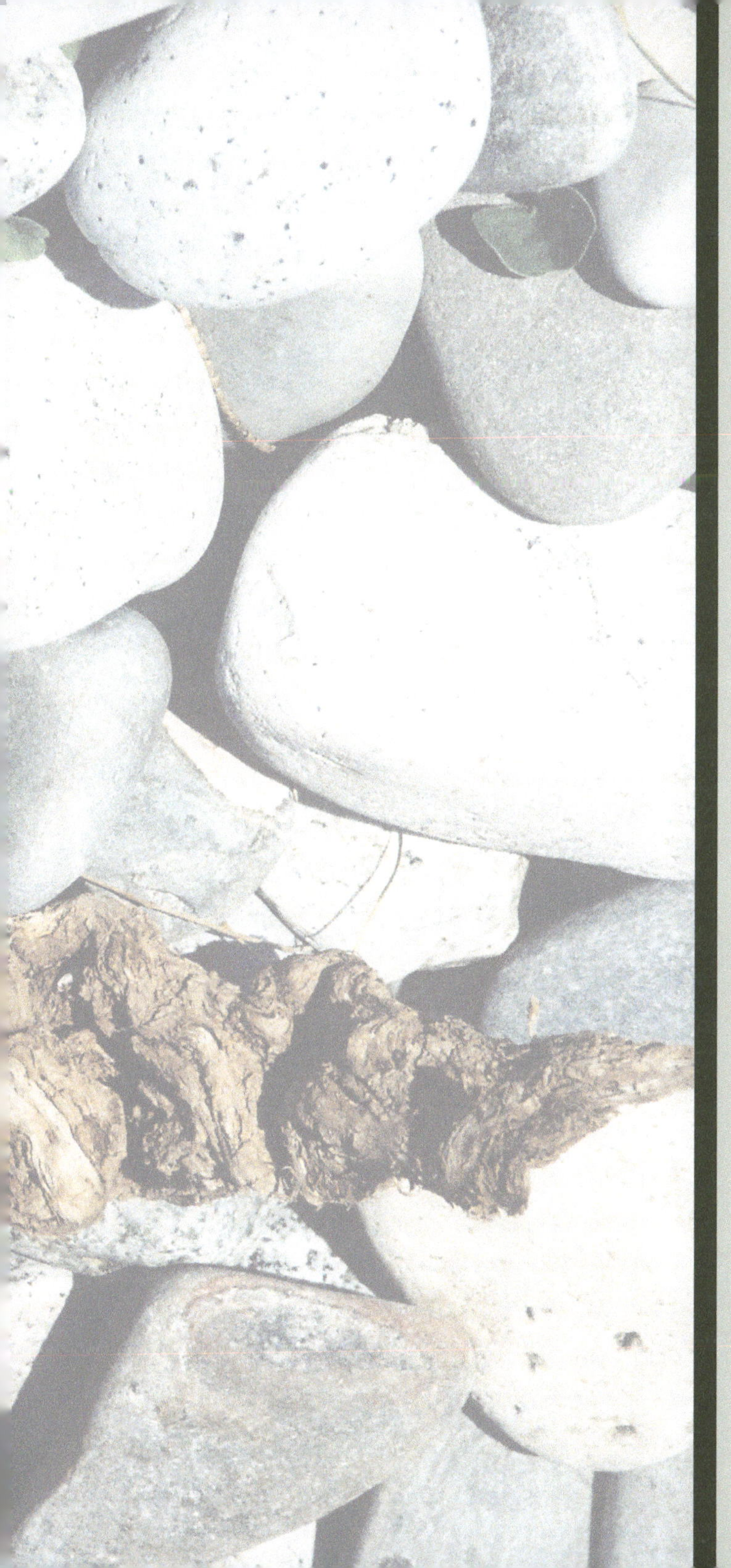

Pebble Poetry
Refining Fire & Light

Next in the Pebble Poetry series is 'Refining Fire & Light', with a matching Canvas Wall Print also available.

Book 2 of the series covers perspectives on eternity, friendships, hope in times of loss and Part 2 of Book 1 poems 'I've Seen …' and 'Welcome'.

Visit www.pebblecollections.com for details.